To my #1 Fan — I love you Anthony !

REVOLVING DOOR

Rose Downing

Revolving Door by Rose M. Downing
Copyright © 2019 Rose M. Downing

All rights reserved. No part of this publication may be reproduced, stored in a retrieval system or transmitted in any form or by any means--electronic, mechanical, digital, recordings, photocopying or any other without prior permission of the publisher.

ISBN - 978-0-578-54960-6

Thank you, God, for my beating heart and the
love that you fill it with daily.
This is a dream realized!

May these words meet you within your heart. May they provide healing or hope, whichever it is that you need for the moment you are in. If you are inspired by my words, feel free to share them with the world. After all, that is @howirose.

P.S. - You are love, in all the ways, always.

Revolving Door

Out of every soul on Earth,

if it isn't yours,

then it holds no worth.

Rose Downing

I tried to move on with somebody new,
but even he said he knows
I'm still a prisoner of you.

Revolving Door

I never could believe every lie that you said.
Every breath that you breathed somehow made me feel dead.
Believing I belonged to the devil the way you had me constantly seeing red.
Your desertion served purpose to my being,
like an exorcism that allowed my heart to start beating.

I can't hold your thoughts of me to be true
when they come from such a filtered point of
view.

Revolving Door

Pick me up and make my million pieces whole,
for you are the one who shattered my soul.
Make it your duty for me to recognize love.
Make me believe this is something we can still
rise above.

Magic like ours doesn't occur twice,

so forgive me if you remain my lifelong vice.

It's a double-edged sword

that I helplessly run toward.

If this chase is what marks my death,

know that I loved you until my very last breath.

Revolving Door

Save me, soft love.

I am meant to feel much more than toughness.

I ache for a love undreamed of,

a heart with passion as my compass.

A place where certainty eliminates all doubt.

A place where I know I'm with the one

I'm not meant to be without.

Hold me close

and listen

to the silence

between the beats of my heart.

Feel the rhythm

and let yourself

reminisce in

the love we shared

before we drifted

a p a r t.

Revolving Door

I can sense every bit of fear
as you ask me not to leave.
Nothing you say can hold me here.
Now is your time to grieve.

Rose Downing

On the sunset under which I take my final
breath,
I'll leave knowing that we still had love left.
I pray next life when we meet once more,
that together we live out the love we both long
for.

Revolving Door

Knowing the chase will leave me empty,
how much of this void will I try to fill?

We are alone in this room
and I look around as you seek to consume.
I feel your growing desire to prey.
I can no longer resist, I never break away.
You grab me, and to your arms I unfold in.
I've never discovered a silence that felt this
golden.

Revolving Door

There is an immense pressure in my chest that I can't quite explain.
I feel it in your presence, I feel it at the mention of your name.
I often wonder if I'll ever break free,
from the soul inside of you that haunts the soul inside of me.

Run fast and burn the bridge behind you.

There is nothing left that we can salvage.

Life spent and time wasted,

holding onto a love that forever remains tainted.

Revolving Door

As my days come to an end,

whether they were grey or they were blue,

there was no way I could pretend

that my mind wandered to anyone other than

you.

As our days of division kept multiplying,

my heart grew content

no longer denying,

the taste of our love was no longer satisfying.

Rose Downing

You took flight from my heart.
You traveled fast, we were miles apart.
It took you longer than I expected,
but now you're back and shocked to find
yourself getting rejected.
While you were gone, I made peace with your desertion.
I moved on and became a much better person.

Revolving Door

Surrender your body
and sink into mine.
Within these four walls
is where we truly
shine, baby shine.

Rose Downing

When the rhythm of your heart no longer has a beat,

what will I have but the world beneath my feet?

Revolving Door

What a monster you must be
to come rip the soul right out of me.
What sick and twisted games you must play
to tell me you don't love me,
yet you never stay away.

Rose Downing

What we were
and what we each could be,
was never able to thrive,
until we both broke free.

Revolving Door

I'm crying out into the dead of night.
When will the good Lord make things right?

Rose Downing

Your rejection

was my redirection.

    - going south was never my calling.

Revolving Door

Sealed up and locked out,
I've bolted my heart's door.
You're driving your wedge,
penetrating like never before.
How will I ever move on,
if you are always leaving
but never stay gone?

Rose Downing

Even though I've grown numb to you,

I can't seem to move on to a love that is new.

I've got no time for trial and error.

I've been through it all before,

with you as my preparer.

Revolving Door

Is this life,

that is lacking love,

what is destined for me?

Please tell me otherwise.

Please, make me believe.

Rose Downing

There's not much I associate to you anymore.
I let it all go when you ripped out my heart
and left it to rot on the floor.
Now I'm walking around as cold as can be,
always asking myself if love is really for me.
My new mindset,
I must admit,
is ruthless.
Encouraging my heart
to forever remain rootless.

Revolving Door

How can it feel both familiar and brand new?
As I lay here making love to you.
How can your scent take me back to our beginning?
Before we lost it all, before you left me reminiscing.

I'm forever bonded to part of your soul.
Forced to move on, will I ever feel whole?

Revolving Door

Tear drops on my pillow case
from a love I can't erase.
What is it that'll get me through?
I lost it all when I lost you.

Rose Downing

Sometimes what we want most
is the very thing that hinders our growth.
I've wished and I've hoped,
but at this very moment I'm at the end of my rope.
The love we had is dead and gone,
I know now that I must move on.
With this farewell comes relief,
no more false hope, no more belief.

Revolving Door

Time doesn't heal unless you move along with it.
And I can't accept this change when my heart is still committed.

Rose Downing

Driving fast in the carbon black

on a one way street.

I'm never going back.

Revolving Door

One day I will erase you
and replace you,
just like you did to me.

They say what goes around comes around.
So, who would I be
if I played your game another round
robbing karma of performing to the fullest
degree?

Rose Downing

When holding on is all I know,
I'm blind to the strength of letting go.
Until I completely free myself I'll never see
that there is so much more than you buried
inside of me.

Revolving Door

Your words,
although plenty,
ring empty.
Your touch,
although steady,
feels weak.
Your heart,
although present,
pumps doubt.
All reassuring me
I am someone
that you can always
live without.

The absence of your love was once haunting.
Now I can honestly say you're not the one I'm wanting.
But the thing that frightens me the most,
is that I no longer feel your ghost.

Revolving Door

You broke me.

And if I let go of the idea that repair can occur,

maybe I'll find a way to be.

In a place where my mind doesn't feel a blur,

maybe I'll find a way to be.

If I can find the love that is greater for myself,

maybe I'll find a way to be.

Rose Downing

I look back and realize
that I lost so much of me
while holding onto you.

Revolving Door

Please stay away.

So that all of my pieces can learn to be.

You play games with my heart and it slowly decays.

Don't pretend it is something you can't see.

Rose Downing

There are too many reasons why our love fell
apart.
We're in this place and I can't deny
our only healing is in a new start.

Revolving Door

It hurts the most when the reasons are unexplainable.
We're so caught between closure and the unattainable.

Rose Downing

Cut the cord and call it a day,
I never wished to merely survive this way.

Revolving Door

Cross my boundaries
and pull me back into yours.
Our intimate bond allows moments of ease,
even if it never goes beyond our bedroom doors.

Rose Downing

I let my entire self bleed out
for you to witness my love.

Revolving Door

I can't get you out of my mind.
What happened to the healing power of time?

Rose Downing

After all of this time,
I never believed
that the choice was mine.
So you come and you go,
I get high and go low.

How long will I
dance with destruction
before I break free
from the man
who's killing me?

Revolving Door

The horror that haunted the halls of our home exposed us to so much that our hearts never should have known.

Rose Downing

I don't love you like I once did.
I cut myself off, put my heart on forbid.
Understand it wasn't something I ever wanted,
but a route I had to take before my soul
completely rotted.

I could forget it all and try to press forward,
or I could face it head on and demolish my own
borders.
You see, I'd rather deal with the pain of coming
to closure,
than to live the rest of my life missing out on
true love's exposure.

Revolving Door

The outcome from what we think we know
is the only way to help us grow.
Maybe you giving all you knew to me
was to bring you to the place you were truly
meant to be.

My heart doesn't question what can you do for me,
I simply want to give love and let love be my key.
I want to unlock the truth inside of your being,
and seal our bond with a much deeper meaning.

Revolving Door

I tried to move forward
but can't seem to find
what the doctor ordered.
    - love sick

There is so much more lingering in the labyrinth
my soul calls home.
Follow your inner compass and you shall see,
I've surrendered these layers for only you to
roam.

Revolving Door

Each night that goes by,
I am alone.
I sit and think of all of the ways
that I have grown.
Even in the time that passes,
I may never surpass his
expectations of me
and all that he
wanted me to be.

You were like anesthesia to my soul.
Putting me under, losing all control.

We drifted to a place most will never see.
Where nothing else existed, just you and me.

Now that I've awoken,
I don't know how to feel.

I'm numb to it all,
still in denial that this is real.

I stare into your innocent eyes through a photograph.
And in that moment, I am capable of erasing our tragic aftermath.

Then our reality quickly takes hold in lieu,
as a harsh reminder that I could never complete you.

Revolving Door

You are a habit
I can't seem to break.

No
body
else
feels
like
you.

I lay here naked, as vulnerable as can be.
You stand at the edge of the bed, but I can
already feel you sink into me.

The slow, passionate love we make
is never enough to replace the swift exit you
take.

So when it's all said and done and you're once
again gone,
I pull myself up and put my dignity back on.

How can a love that started in such simplicity
leave me soaking in the absence of a man who
lacks the authenticity
to stick to his decision to leave regardless of
what he can come back and get away with?
He'd rather keep me on a shelf like some shiny
toy he just likes to play with.

Revolving Door

I cannot let go of anything
until I am forced by what has let go of me.

Rose Downing

I can exhaust all efforts as protection to my core;
Yet, I can never find a strong enough sealant,
to stop you from destroying me more.

Revolving Door

Your touch once said everything
that you couldn't articulate.
Now your fingertips leave a sting
from the love you let dissipate.

Rose Downing

Increase the intake
and I still don't get my fix.

Revolving Door

There is one thing I know,
it's the sadness, tears and heartache
that taught me how to grow.

Rose Downing

I want to give you my love
but I don't know where to start.

There is blockage in my veins
and nothing can pump through to my heart.

Our painful past is preventing me
from giving you my soul, from loving entirely.

Revolving Door

There is no destination,
no mile marker three.
Just endless restoration
on the road built for finding me.

Rose Downing

I cannot convince you to stay,
the door is open and you're out halfway.
Your eyes tell me without a single word
that your heart is leaving mine,
it is being transferred.

Revolving Door

I should have walked away
when you said you needed time
to know if you wanted to stay.

I try to cut you out of my life in every way.
Inside of my soul is where you seem to stay.

Every night I end up in thoughts of you,
as if some sort of ritual.
I can't help but analyze the mess we got into
or begin to understand why this hurt remains
continual.

Revolving Door

Love gets me so high,
you're the only one who can bring the supply.

But the only thing that gets me sober,
is knowing you'll once again tell me this is over.

They say you can't undo what has been done.
So how can I unlove the man I believed was the one?

Revolving Door

You prey on my flesh,

but forget how to feed my soul.

How dare you be so selfish

leaving me to do the damage control?

Rose Downing

After all of the hurt I've had to rise above,
I can't blame my heart for being reluctant.
It's not that I don't believe in love,
it's that I don't trust my own judgement.

Revolving Door

3 a.m. and I roll over to check my phone.
What is it about me that hates sleeping alone?

Rose Downing

All of these years have passed and I still can't forget,
losing your love has been my biggest regret.

Revolving Door

I want to run far away from the consumption of
our lost love
and put an end to the fix-it scenarios that I
continuously dream of.

Rose Downing

Pour out the bottle and I pour out my thoughts.
I miss you terribly which is something that can't
be stopped.
I'm weak for you and want you in my life,
even if my confession only follows these drinks
tonight.

Revolving Door

I put on my shield,
ready to protect my heart
through any field.

Once again the battle of me
leaving you approaches
and instead of fighting through,
I somehow become clothe less.
As we lay in bed making love outside of our war,
I can't help but wonder if I'll ever stop wanting more.

Our break may have broke me,
but the false hope you dangled in front of me
time and time again is what destroyed me.

Why wasn't it you
who brought me
back to life?

Revolving Door

They say give credit where credit is due,
so the heartbreak is where
I must acknowledge you.

Rose Downing

We are a dream
trapped
in a nightmare.

When does this rope
stop unraveling?

Revolving Door

It wasn't me that you were escaping.
It was from the depths of your own soul
of which you needed saving.

Rose Downing

Forever true

is the love I have with you.

No matter what time or place,

it can never be replaced.

In this life now

and within each one after,

I pray we find a way

to finally master,

the soulful love

that was always sent from above.

Revolving Door

I look around and seek to take flight,

to travel back to when things between us felt right.

For some reason I remain stuck here, and I know you would agree,

that no road can travel back to the old you and me.

Rose Downing

The complexity of our physical chemistry,

the two of us, make ecstasy.

It's heavily heavenly

yet messily mentally.

Our bodies perform

a tentative intensity,

yet our minds

forever seek

a restful remedy.

Revolving Door

You hallowed me out right from the core
and while my soul feels alone,
my body stays aching for more.

You can find me where the skies are blue.
Ready to give my best to you.

Revolving Door

Drink a bottle down

and suddenly I feel weaker.

We've been apart some time now,

but I feel myself becoming the same old seeker.

Rose Downing

Lost in the darkness

I can't find my way back.

I'm crippled from the ways we fell under attack.

    - love grenade

Revolving Door

How many times will I try to drink and drown
the reality that you're nowhere to be found?

The truth coming to light
buried me in darkness.

Revolving Door

You may have put out the fire,

but my scars still remain.

After all that has transpired,

my heart will never feel the same.

Rose Downing

I'm so good at running and hiding,
nobody would know that losing you
has me nearly flat lining.

Revolving Door

Looking at you hurts
almost as much
as the emptiness
I taste when we kiss.
But instead of walking away,
I tread the outskirts
of our chaotic love's
deep abyss.

Rose Downing

The place I sought solace,

only left me more soulless.

Still, your abandoning arms make the best love.

Revolving Door

Letting down our guards was dangerous.
We kept hurting each other, it was engrained in us.

Do you ever think
we should have remained a thought?

Rose Downing

The ocean of my tears allowed me to swim
from a stranded island to the safest shore.

Revolving Door

I surrender to you and let our bodies collide.
It's a price that I pay to feel so alive.

Rose Downing

I was willing to endure all of the stings
just to have tastes of your honey.

Revolving Door

I just want our truths to touch.

He whispers, "You can't even tell me you don't want me."

She replies, "That is in fact what has cost me, me."

Revolving Door

Touch me tender.

Until, in all the ways, I surrender.

Rose Downing

I keep forgetting to forget you.

Revolving Door

I can't erase you,
there's no way to.
You are a piece of me,
I'll love you forever, indefinitely.

Rose Downing

I don't want closure
because closure means that all of this is over.
And if I can't make love to you,
there is a withdrawal that I'll go through.
I know that we share the same addiction,
so I hope you feel this with all of my conviction.

"Please don't do this to me,
please don't leave," I beg and plead.
You are mine and I am yours.
I mean that now like never before.

Revolving Door

I can reach out for you, but I can't seem to touch.
I can get close to you, but I can't seem to feel your love.
I just wish I could defy gravity.
Meet you in a place where we didn't hurt each other this badly.

How did our love become a catastrophe?

Rose Downing

These hands won't continue to dig up what is
already dead.
As if I hold the power to bring back a love
that can no longer bleed
after all that it bled.

Revolving Door

Like the gravitational pull, I'll always hold you down.

Rose Downing

Forgive me, it took me this long to forgive.

Revolving Door

Burnt moments in our memory.
We were each other's pain,
and somehow too,
each other's remedy.

Rose Downing

Nobody else's words
puncture me
quite like yours.

You hurt me,
broken,
but I healed whole.

Revolving Door

Your demons play well with mine.
Hence why I run back to you during our dark times.

Rose Downing

You
are
the
only
thing
missing
between
close
and
closure.

Revolving Door

You had me so open, but your motives were hidden.
I sacrificed it all for you and some days I wish I didn't.

Rose Downing

Your raging waters came over me like a hurricane.
The most violent of storms,
I wasn't prepared for such pain.

Revolving Door

loverstrangers

    - we didn't miss a beat

Rose Downing

If it takes two to tango, it's only right that I take half of this blame.
If all is fair in love and war, is it a draw since we're one and the same?

Revolving Door

I couldn't continue to swallow the pill on the script that you wrote.
You prescribed the pain, not the antidote.

I've hardened my heart.

It's my protection.

It's my art.

Revolving Door

I never was good at being eloquent with you,
but because of this hurt, I can write the hell out
of you.

Rose Downing

I stand by this bed at attention,

ready to do anything that you mention.

Because in some twisted way,

I think this physical addiction will get you to

stay.

Revolving Door

Consider all that you've dished out,

is that a pill you'd be prepared to swallow?

And if I chose another man over you without any doubt,

would it have you feeling heartbroken and hollow?

Rose Downing

What is it about you

that prevents me

from

maintaining

any form of recovery?

Revolving Door

When the current no longer moves you,
tell me, what happens to the flow?

And if I sink into my own shadows,
will you have the courage to be my light?
    - for better and for worse

Rose Downing

Come close and hold me.
Let love encompass our beings.
Let us form together as one,
rest in our self-made cocoon
until our spirits are ready
for the ultimate metamorphosis.
When we return to love
we will only know light.

Revolving Door

You're intoxicatingly toxic.
I know I should quit, but I can't stop it.

I just don't know how I never knew.
- in denial of my own intuition

Revolving Door

I just want to be close to you.
What is a girl supposed to do?
    - I can't move on

Wherever you are,
I hope you are ok.
I can't draw you near,
but in my heart, you are always at bay.
I know it may be wrong, but was our timing ever right?
I was hoping if I send my location, you'd be down to meet up tonight.
There's a concrete ocean between us
but we've got some unfinished business.
Would you pound the pavement to come release one last time?
Does your heart still race when the thought of me comes to your mind?

Revolving Door

My heart felt your explosive love.
And my God,
it has left me wounded.

Rose Downing

Stick to this beat
Baby, stay with me.
I've always believed
in the make believe.

Revolving Door

Maybe,

love was always us.

Maybe,

love was never enough.

Rose Downing

The rush of your love comes over me the way
the waves meet the shore.

As if meant to cover all of me, soaking my sands
before drifting back to sea.

Although I know that you ebb and flow, I'm
never ready for you to leave.

Revolving Door

I lost a love in the city.
Letting go of you
meant finding me.

I question the veracity of everything you state.
Why is it so hard for you to feel your feels and
with me, keep it straight?

Revolving Door

We're merely existing in the same space
without love, not a single trace.
    - how did we get here?

Rose Downing

Our love is locked and loaded, explosive.
Maybe I'm only meant to have you in doses.

Revolving Door

An old playlist, a little bit of wine
and suddenly I'm right back in time.
See how easy it is to set the mood?
One thought of you and my entire mind you
intrude.
I'm reminiscent of
the way we made love.
The way we'd break-up
even better than make-up.
It was all so cyclical,
yet somewhat rhythmical.
You always knew just how to strum my chords,
to your arms I was constantly running towards.
It was an endless fix
and I wanted to feel good even though I knew
I'd end up being kicked.

Kicked down. Down to the bottom.
Like the bottom of this bottle.
Man, forget reminiscing, this much liquid has
got me feeling hostile.
See it's all because of you,
all of this pain that I've been through.

And if we're pointing fingers
then I'm aiming at the man who makes it all still linger.

Your poison fills the blood that runs through my veins.
It weighs so heavy, I'm internally chained.
This isn't some beautiful medley, it's messy.
You and I both know it's safe to say, this love is deadly.

Revolving Door

I can no longer
hurt for you.

Rose Downing

You had me at hello.
Like a stick up show and my heart had to go.
You ripped it out without any mercy
knowing, I'd roam this Earth and for you,
forever remaining thirsty.

Revolving Door

A satisfaction that I seek
leaves me forever weak.

Pain that isn't transformed is transmitted.
That's why all of your demons have me feeling conflicted.
Loving on you while you suck the life right out of me,
my mind is so lost in the perplexity.
It's like you won't stay gone
until you see the last drop of blood leave from my heart.
Doesn't it hurt to see me so withdrawn?
Knowing the pain you've inflicted played the biggest part?
If leaving you is right, dare I be wrong?
Is your heart really where mine belongs?
This feels so distorted.
A line between us hit some type of shortage.
You're in front of me but nothing seems clear,
and my heart hurts because I just wanted you near.

Revolving Door

Body to body wasn't enough,
why was keeping you always so tough?

Spent endless nights wrapped up in you,
knowing my kind was deep in too.

I openly sacrificed my heart
not knowing how fast my world would fall
apart.

Cut open and broken down,
still the only thing I wanted was for you to stick
around.

Your corrupt ways and all they elicited,
weighed heavier than any desire I had which
could have fixed it.

The story was written before I even knew,
and all that we endured, I needed to go through.

Your curse was my gift, it truly shaped me.
For that alone, I forever thank you, baby.

Rose Downing

It's like we switched roles
and here I stand, unable to console.
You're hung up on me now that it's over.
How does it feel not to gain closure?
The victor between you and me
was karma and destiny.
Let this run its course my dear;
there is no more love, no more revere.

Revolving Door

You reach out to me in the dead of night.
Not because your heart wants to come and make this right,
but because your body wishes to feast on the pleasures of mine.
And you know there's still a piece of me that never can decline.

Rose Downing

I tried to compensate
for all of the ways that you fell short,
but this time you've got me in check mate,
and saying goodbye is my last resort.

Revolving Door

Who I wanted you to be
is so far from who you really are.
It just wasn't something I was able to see,
until there was no room left on my heart for
another scar.

Rose Downing

Body to body,

but where is your soul?

Rhetorical, really.

I know it ran away from home.

Revolving Door

Drawn out, a husk is all that is left of me.
The woman I once was,
died trying to love you free.

Rose Downing

Got my head in the clouds

floating back to the image I once had of you.

How'd you drift so far away?

Revolving Door

Useful,
until useless
to you.

Rose Downing

What I know.
What I don't know.
What I should have known.
Maybe, I always knew.

Revolving Door

Can't seem to punch the numbers listening to this dial tone,
it really has me wondering why I even picked up my phone.
Reaching out to you isn't going to make you reroute.
You left home because you were already emotionally checked out.
Why do I keep trying to jump through hoops and play with fire,
when I'll never again be the one who your heart desires?

Rose Downing

Little too drunk,

thinking about that dial.

Hung up on you,

baby it's been a while.

Revolving Door

Pedaling back,

trying to pick up the slack.

We can't undo what has been done.

Maybe you and I were never meant to be one.

You seek out hearts that are easy to break.
What do you do with the souls that you take?

Revolving Door

I hit bottom with the rocks,
still I dream of mountain tops.
If what goes up must come down,
I'll reverse it all until I am found.
Fresh out of the valley and climbing to the peak,
to let darkness overtake me, did you really think
I was that weak?

Flip the switch off and then turn me on.
Make love to me underneath the moon and then hold me until dawn.
My, oh my, not much has changed since you've been gone.
It's your gentle touch that sparks the release.
And in these moments, I forget how you always come back just to rob me of my peace.

Revolving Door

My loyalty to you was so strong
that I couldn't protect myself.

My heart is breaking in the silence.
Tell me where we go from here, I need your guidance,
because you were the one who was always in control.
And now that you've cut me off, I don't know where to call home for my soul.
You see without you, I'm not good at being strong.
Please stay another night with me and just play along.
If there is one way that we know how to get it right,
it is the moments we come together in the darkest of nights.
I know I'm asking you to play with fire,
but you're all I know, it's just how I'm wired.

Revolving Door

Ring the alarm.

He made his way back and is working his charm.

In the past, he could sink me like a ship.

It's what he loved to do, an ego trip.

This time around I won't be targeted.

I stand here new, a heart demarcated.

Rose Downing

I can't remember the last time
you softly spoke those three words;
I love you.

Revolving Door

I say things out of spite

in hopes of you revealing a side that is still

willing to fight.

But once again you show me that you're

through.

Will I ever grow weary of this view?

Of you walking out on me like we're easily over

and done?

Why do you always hide your feelings and run?

Rose Downing

What is it about you that makes me senseless?
It's reckless, it's endless.

Revolving Door

We're taught not to play with fire.
But we're never told
that fire burns deep
in our lover's soul.

About the writer

Rose Downing is a writer and freelance model based in New York City. Her poetry engages themes of love, loss, healing, and power. In sharing her poetry with the world, she hopes to touch many hearts with words they may need to hear. She hopes to spark inspiration in others to express their own stories of healing, growing, and love.

You can find more of her work at:

www.howirose.com